Copyright © 2016 by Stephanie Brown. 737103

ISBN: Softcover   978-1-5144-9642-8
         Hardcover   978-1-5144-9643-5
         EBook   978-1-5144-9722-7

Print information available on the last page

Rev. date: 09/13/2016

To order additional copies of this book, contact:
Xlibris
1-800-455-039
www.xlibris.com.au
Orders@Xlibris.com.au

A Selection of Short Poems

Stephanie Brown

for Jeremy
with love and prayers

For I know the plans I have for you, declares the Lord, plans to prosper you and not to harm you, plans to give you a hope and a future. Then you will call upon me and come and pray to me, and I will listen to you. You will seek me and find me when you seek me with all your heart.

Jeremiah 29: 11-13 (NIV)

4

You

In abundance
You are glorious, beautiful
All creation bows before you,
None but you
is where true life is found.
God is true and real,
All life is found in him

Guidance

An utterance unknown
Your words set in stone.
The tablet bearing your laws
Was made on that mount,
Yet your laws are within our hearts,
Your words in our mouths
That you may be glorified as we are a blessed people,
living under your grace.
Your Holy Spirit within us,
Enabling, encouraging and guiding
'Teach us your ways' man asks
Read my Word!
If we read your word and hear your word and listen to your
direction,
Your way becomes clear,
For you are my enabler.

A mere thank you for that bloodied cross

The blood shed,
The tears run.
In that moment, on that cross
With God's wrath upon him,
Something happened between God and his son
Jesus
That I cannot understand.
But what I do know, his blood covers me
So I now, can enter his presence with joyful thanksgiving,
Remember always to thank my saviour
Alive and living!
For taking my sin and burdens,
Bearing in that moment all the sin of the world.
Jesus Christ died,
Jesus Christ then alive!
I now benefit - to say thank you is not enough,
My life is yours

Life

Life fulfilled, life renewed, restored and victorious
Now in Jesus Christ, conqueror of all
Satisfaction in our Lord,
Joy and love given without condition,
New life, new hope, a purpose and direction.
To find one's identity in Jesus Christ,
The only place it is found.
To all, the invitation,
Come
All who are thirsty,
Come
All who are hungry,
Come to the Lord Jesus
And be filled with true life,
Life found in Him.
Come choose him now.

A new hope

Hope abounds

The heart bursts

Your radiance, brilliant,

your love, perfect and pure

What is this I have found?

No restraint in joyful exclamation to those who have not yet

known

Joy! Peace! Love!

Glorious, almighty, awesome, majestic and magnificent God!

Who rules and reigns,

Everything pales in comparison.

To you I lift my hands in praise and worship,

To God who is everlasting

The Alpha and Omega,

Endless praise and worship is His.

Nearer the end

The clock ticks and time slows,

But it feels fast to me.

The winding up, the chasing down

As the earth dwindles to its inevitable close.

A bright, shining one coming in glory,

But not yet, but not yet

Still many things to be done.

My ear however listens and my eyes watch for the sign of the

times

But not yet, not yet loved one,

Still many things to be done.

Of love lost and found

The turning away
From goodness and great
A foolish man I once knew,
Stumbling in the darkness until one day,
He knew, he knew, a difference to be made
A final gasp, a release of expression
A choice to be had and the correct one taken.
Finally, although not really too long,
Joy, peace and true love found
Born again, in the arms of his saviour,
Jesus Christ.

Grace

What grace has found me,
What grace covers me
What grace but yours alone,
Your grace is sufficient for me.

Majesty

To the ends of the earth
The distant stars,
No-one can fully comprehend you.
Your mysteries abound,
Unfathomable, unsearchable
And yet you chose for a time to be earth bound.
A man and God in one,
So that I might be called a child.

A personal relationship,
A delightful mystery that you are known to me
The benefits, amazing,
Your plan – perfect.

Shining

We are but fleeting.
May we, if just for a moment,
Consider you.
So that your light shines through us to others,
For we are but grass on the field,
Here today and gone tomorrow.
Our home is in heaven,
We are your ambassadors
So let us consider you,
So that your light may shine through us to others,
That they too be on the path to you,
And be your ambassadors, shining your light.

In his heart a man plans his course, but the Lord determines his steps.

Proverbs 16:9 (NIV)

For I know the plans I have for you, declares the Lord, plans to prosper you and not to harm you, plans to give you a hope and a future. Then you will call upon me and come and pray to me, and I will listen to you. You will seek me and find me when you seek me with all your heart.

Jeremiah 29: 11-13 (NIV)

Thank you firstly to God and all my family, natural and spiritual for your constant love and prayers.